It's another Quality Book from CGP

This Teacher Book is perfect for helping you get the most out of CGP's Year 6 Word Power Book.

It contains a huge range of useful teaching resources, including example answers to each question, extra background material, suggestions for scaffolding and extension activities... plus much more.

What CGP is all about

Our sole aim here at CGP is to produce the highest quality books — carefully written, immaculately presented and dangerously close to being funny.

Then we work our socks off to get them out to you — at the cheapest possible prices.

Do You Mind If I Borrow That?

2 *Section 1 — Change And Exchange*

Do You Mind If I Borrow That?

Extra Background

English has borrowed words from many different languages across the world, but some languages have also borrowed words from English. French, for example, has borrowed 'le week-end', 'le jogging' and 'le sport'.

Pupil Guidance

Some borrowed words may seem exotic because they have spelling patterns that are not common in English. The letter 'k' isn't that common in English unless it's used with another letter in a consonant cluster (e.g. 'sk' and 'ck').

Extension Idea

Ask students to investigate the links between Britain and India. The English language has many words that come from Hindi and Urdu. Then ask students to consider why this might be. Reasons could include the number of people who have emigrated from India to England, and the influence of the British Empire.

Languages don't exist in their own little bubbles. Instead, they're constantly exchanging words. English has been influenced by loads of other languages.

Loan words are words that have been borrowed from another language.

Here are some loan words in English, and where they come from.

Australia	America	India	Japan	Middle East
kangaroo	canoe	bungalow	tsunami	bazaar
budgerigar	powwow	gymkhana	karaoke	caravan
boomerang	hurricane	jungle	judo	giraffe

Are you surprised that all of these words come from other languages? Would you say they feel exotic? If so, how?

Look at the pairs of words below. Which word in each pair do you think has been borrowed from another language? Circle the 'borrowed' words.

 (kayak) boat   (pyjamas) nightwear   (shampoo) soap

house (igloo)   storm (typhoon)   waterproof (anorak)

How did you identify the borrowed words? Write down your thoughts below.

✎ Some of them are words that don't have familiar spellings, but others are words that I know come from elsewhere, like igloo.

English has borrowed words from all across the world. How do you think the English language has ended up with words from so far afield?

What do you know about where British people have travelled and settled in history?

✎ I know that people in Britain travelled widely around the world, and there were lots of British explorers. I think explorers brought some words back, but also people who came to live here brought their own words with them.

Extension Idea

We are still picking up new words in English all the time, especially for foods. Students may wish to ask others, especially adults, if they have eaten 'papaya', 'daal' or 'chorizo'.

Do You Mind If I Borrow That? — Aims:

- to introduce pupils to the concept of borrowed words
- to understand how and why English borrowed words from other languages
- to reflect on the reasons for language change and acquisition of words into the English language.

3

Borrowed words often have quite specific meanings. This is great, because this meaning might be exactly what you're looking for. Find out the meanings of the loan words below.

Do you know which language any of these words are from?

vigilante ➡ someone who tries to stop crime, who isn't a policeman

frisson ➡ a strong feeling

replica ➡ an exact copy

People have been borrowing words for centuries. In the 1500s, when the Spanish and the Portuguese took over most of South America, they took their languages with them.

The people who already lived in Central and South America had their own languages. The Aztecs and the Haitians spoke their own languages, such as Nahuatl and Arawak. These languages started to influence Spanish and Portuguese — and vice versa!

When the Spanish and Portuguese went home to Europe, they took some South American foods with them. These foods came with new words.

Psst... try removing the 'h' from the last one.

The red words below are in Nahuatl. The green words are in Arawak. Can you work out which English words these words have become?

xocolatl   tomatl   chilli   papáia   mahiz
chocolate, tomato, chilli, papaya, maize

Why do you think there were no words for these foods in European languages?

Because we didn't have these foods until they were introduced into this country by people coming back from South America.

What have you learned on these pages about borrowed words in English?

I've learnt that borrowed words have come from other languages, and that a lot of food words are borrowed.

Pupil Guidance

'Vigilante' comes from the Spanish word meaning 'watchman' or 'guard'. 'Frisson' comes from a French word meaning 'a shiver', and 'replica' is from Italian, meaning 'to reply' or 'to repeat'.

Extension Idea

Put a world map on the wall, and ask students to decorate it with pictures of all the foods they can think of that are not originally from the UK.

Suggested Scaffolding

This could be quite an abstract concept for some pupils. A lead-in question might be, 'What would happen if someone came back from South America and held out a papaya, and then their friend asked them what it was?'

Pupil Guidance

Pupils may also choose to list words that they didn't realise were borrowed.

Worldwide Words

4

Worldwide Words

Thanks to modern technology, people around the world can communicate more easily than ever before. This can affect the languages people want to speak.

Here are a few inventions that help communication in the modern world:

Internet   email   video messaging   smartphones   cheap air travel

Pick one or two of these inventions and explain how you think it has made communication easier.

Internet: People across the world can read the same things and communicate instantly.
Cheap air travel: People can visit different countries cheaply.

In Britain, we don't make all the products we need — we need to buy some things (like some foods) from other countries. In exchange, we sell them the things that we make. This is called trade. When countries trade, they need to decide what language to trade in!

It's often said that if you want to buy something, you can usually speak your own language, but if you want to sell something, you have to speak the customer's language. Why do you think this is?

To buy something you just need to hand over the money, but to sell you need to persuade someone to spend money. It's easier to persuade people using their own language.

Choose two languages you think might be important for trade, and explain why.

Which countries make lots of products?
Which languages are spoken worldwide?

Language 1:   English   Important because: lots of films and music are produced in America and England and shown across the world.

Language 2:   Mandarin   Important because: there is lots of industry in China so I think they trade quite a lot.

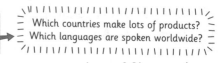

Worldwide Words — Aims:

- to develop pupils' understanding of global word exchange and the means by which it happens
- to consider the reasons why one language might become more widely used than others
- to reflect on the status and protection of less commonly spoken languages.

5

Having some languages that lots of people speak across the world is very handy for trade, but people are also keen to protect <u>minority languages</u>.

What do you think a 'minority language' is? Can you think of any examples?

I think 'minority language' means ✎ a language which is spoken by a small number of people in a country.

Examples might be: ✎ Breton in France, and Cornish and Manx.

Why might people be keen to protect the languages they speak?

✎ Your language is part of who you are.

Also if people stopped speaking your language you'd probably have to learn another one, and that might be tricky.

> Think about what your language means to you.

Read the speech bubble below.

> I think there should only be one language spoken across the whole world.

> You may want to include some of your answers from the question above, but try to think of other reasons why only speaking one language might not be a good idea.

Write down some arguments 'for' and 'against' people only speaking one language.

For	Against
✎ Trade would be simpler if everyone spoke the same language. It would be easier to visit foreign countries on holiday. There would be fewer misunderstandings between people from different countries.	✎ It would be tricky to decide which language to pick. Everybody across the world would have to learn a new language. People might get upset if their old language became extinct.

What do you now know about languages in the modern world, that you didn't know before?

✎ I know that some languages are spoken in a lot of places, but there are also many minority languages in the world.

Section 1 — Change And Exchange

Extra Background

Languages can be classified as 'endangered'. Cornish is considered to be 'severely endangered'.

Suggested Scaffolding

Ask children to think about how they would feel if their class was the only group of English speakers left in the world.

Suggested Scaffolding

To help children come up with the 'for' arguments, it might be helpful to imagine that English had been picked as the new global language. To help children come up with the 'against' arguments, it might be helpful for pupils to imagine an unfamiliar language, such as Swahili, had been chosen.

Pupil Guidance

Losing languages could also mean losing specialist knowledge and ideas, especially if these cannot be accurately translated into the new language. For example the German word 'Kummerspeck' means 'the excess weight gained from overeating when you're sad'. (It translates as 'grief bacon'.)

Extension Idea

This is a good subject for a debate. Compile everyone's pros and cons, and then get students to write a speech for one side or the other. This could help pupils practise their argumentative writing and speaking skills.

Language From Literature

Extra Background

Shakespeare was an actor as well as a playwright. He knew he had to make his words entertain and amuse an audience who would have thrown rotten fruit at him if they didn't like his plays.

Pupil Guidance

Before providing dictionaries, encourage students to try to work out what the unfamiliar words might mean using the context of the passage.

Pupil Guidance

Remind pupils that the suffixes '-ise', '-ify' and '-ate' turn nouns into verbs. The suffixes '-ence', '-ance' and 'ation' turn verbs into nouns.

Extension Idea

Pupils could create a 'Book of Shakespearean words', or a display. Get pupils to research some more words that Shakespeare created.

6

Language From Literature

Sometimes it takes hundreds of years for a language to change, but individuals can also add to languages with exciting new words used in new ways.

William Shakespeare is a famous English writer, who lived between 1564-1616. Shakespeare is credited with adding lots of words to the English language. Some of these words he made up completely. With others, he was just the first person to write them down.

All the words in red in this passage were first used by Shakespeare. Do you know what they mean? Look up any you don't know, and write their meanings below.

The airless, characterless prison was too hot. Outside, countless men sneaked past the window. Eric tried to elbow his way outside, but he was bedazzled by the glare of the Sun.

✎ airless — stuffy; characterless — without personality; countless — too many to count; sneaked — to walk in a stealthy way; elbow — to nudge people out of the way using your elbows; bedazzle — to be overcome by brightness

Shakespeare loved to change the categories of words. Previously, 'torture' was used as a noun, but Shakespeare turned it into a verb.

I was tortured by the smell of turnips.

Try changing the categories of words, just like Shakespeare. Choose some nouns and verbs, then try using the nouns as verbs, and the verbs as nouns. Then write some sentences using your new words.

It works best if you pick some fairly <u>unusual</u> words!

Nouns
extravagance
✎ concrete, justice, spider

Verbs
✎ greet, prowl, tumble

✎ "I have been extravagancing too long — it's time I did some work."
Hannah spidered me into cheating on my test.
He needs to be justicised for that behaviour.
The fox's prowlations had trapped the hen by the wall.

Section 1 — Change And Exchange

Suggested Scaffolding

Pupils who are less sure of word classes could write their original words on cards, and try matching them with different suffix cards. Ask them to explain what their new word means before they write a sentence.

Language From Literature — Aims:

- to investigate the effect Shakespeare had on the English language
- to consider how new words may be derived from existing words by changing word classes
- to investigate how writers can leave a lasting impression on a language.

Shakespeare also created lots of insults — some of them might seem a bit strange to us today.

Thou cream-faced loon!

Away, you cutpurse rascal!

A cutpurse is a pickpocket.

Use the words below to create some insults of your own in Shakespeare's style.

lily-livered — cowardly
impertinent — rude
rotten — horrible
poisonous — nasty
saucy — cheeky
loon — crazy person

scoundrel — a cheat
salamander — a lizard
away/begone — go away
verily — truly

mouse   catfish

bean   bowl of soup

cucumber   frog   apple pie

Begone, you saucy salamander!

Verily, you are a rotten bean!

You are a lily-livered scoundrel!

Away with you, poisonous catfish!

He's an impertinent cucumber!

Some of Shakespeare's words didn't catch on at all. Below are some examples of words he created that were only ever used once or twice. Can you match each word to its definition?

questrist   a dessert made from random ingredients

overstink   to smell stronger than something else

misdread   a person who searches for another

hodge-pudding   fear of evil

How did you work out what these words meant?

Another of Shakespeare's words that didn't catch on was 'carlot' — meaning 'peasant'. At this time, there were already several words that meant 'peasant', such as 'villein', 'churl' and 'serf'. Why do you think a writer might create a new word rather than using one that already exists?

Because they want to make their writing more interesting and memorable.

How can people who are creative with words have a lasting impact on a language?

They can add words and phrases to a language, especially if they are a popular writer.

Section 1 — Change And Exchange

Extra Background

Shakespeare did create some entirely new words, but others he created by adding prefixes ('unaware') or making compounds ('cream-faced').

Pupil Guidance

Pupils should be able to spot synonyms in the words and their meanings: 'quest' and 'search'; 'stink' and 'smell'; 'dread' and 'fear'; and 'pudding' and dessert'.

Pupil Guidance

There's no right or wrong answer to this question. Pupils might say that authors create new words to be more precise — the existing words might not have quite the same meaning. Or they might recognise that poets might create new words that have a certain number of syllables or a certain sound to match the metre of the poem.

Extension Idea

Pupils can research other authors or books that have added (or popularised) words in English — J.K. Rowling and the 'Harry Potter' series of books provides lots of good examples.

Standing The Test Of Time

Extra Background

Slang is one of the most rapidly changing parts of English. It's more often spoken than written down, so it can be short-lived.

Extension Idea

There should be a variety of answers here, which could form an interesting class discussion. See if there are matches between pupils who are close friends, and ask them why this might be.

Suggested Scaffolding

Ask pupils if they would <u>expect</u> a word like 'wicked' to be used as a slang word for 'good'.

Suggested Scaffolding

Ask pupils to give an example of when they recently used slang. Does their example fall into any of these categories?

Pupil Guidance

Pupils may give different answers. Discuss any different responses as a group.

Standing The Test Of Time

Some words seem to be with us for good — it's hard to imagine life without words like "bread", "yes" and... well... "and". But others can mysteriously go out of fashion... only to reappear somewhere completely unexpected.

Words are always moving in and out of fashion, especially slang words. These are very informal words used by certain groups of people — like you and your friends, for example. The words below are all words for 'good' from the last 100 years.

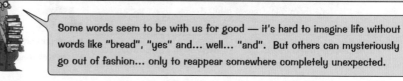

"Ripping!" — 1920s "Groovy!" / "Wicked!" — 1960s "Sweet!" — 1990s Today

What slang word do you use today to mean 'good'? Fill in the speech bubble above.

'Ripping', 'groovy' and 'wicked' all meant something else before 'good', and they still have other meanings. Words can gain and change meanings all the time.

What do these words mean literally? Look them up in a dictionary. What differences do you notice between their slang meanings and their other meanings?

Ripping means tearing. Something groovy has little channels cut into it. Wicked means evil. Sometimes the meanings are negative even though their slang meanings suggest good things.

Why do you think people use slang? Tick all the boxes that apply.

- [x] To sound cool.
- [x] To talk secretly about something.
- [ ] To sound more formal.
- [x] To fit in with other people who use slang.
- [ ] To sound more grown-up.
- [x] It's easier or quicker than talking properly.

Section 1 — Change And Exchange　　　　　　　　*© CGP — not to be photocopied*

Extension Idea

Pupils could make a dictionary of slang, asking adults of different ages which words they used as young people. See if any of them are linked to the period (e.g. 'groovy' refers to the music of the time).

Standing The Test Of Time — Aims:

- to get pupils to recognise that words change, gain and lose meanings over time
- to look at slang as a particularly transient part of the English language
- to reflect on how, and why, words fall in and out of common usage.

We often need new words for new inventions. Sometimes we create these by bringing back very old words (or bits of them!) from languages like Latin and Ancient Greek.

Here are some words that came from Latin and Ancient Greek. Can you think of any names of modern inventions that use them? Write them down in the box below.

Greek
tele
skopein
phone
elektro

Latin
mobilis
computare
video
movere

microscope
computer
telephone
mobile phone
automobile
television
electricity   movie   video player

You may need to change the Latin and Greek spellings.

Why do you think some new inventions are given names from Latin and Ancient Greek?

Because even though these words have been around for thousands of years they're still relevant to modern inventions.

Some words don't just change meaning — they fall out of use altogether.

Can you work out what these words mean?

Use a dictionary or the Internet to help you.

pelisse ➡ a type of cloak

brabble ➡ to argue about things that don't really matter

trencher ➡ a plate made of wood, metal or bread

grumpish ➡ being grumpy and moaning about things a lot

Why do you think these words have died out?

We don't use the object any more, or we use a different word.

What have you learnt about how language changes over time?

Slang words change languages because they give words new meanings. Some words fall out of use over time.

Extension Idea
Challenge pupils to find out what these Latin and Ancient Greek words meant originally.

Suggested Scaffolding
You may want to give pupils the more recognisable versions: 'scope', 'electro', 'mobile', 'computer' and 'move'.

Pupil Guidance
Pupils may give lots of answers to this question. They may say that Latin and Ancient Greek words have been borrowed into several languages, so modern inventions that have Latin and Ancient Greek names are widely understood.

Nouns often fall out of use because we no longer use the object (e.g. 'trencher' and 'pelisse'). Other words may simply have been replaced by a more popular synonym (e.g. 'squabble' rather than 'brabble'; 'grumpy' rather than 'grumpish').

Extension Idea
Provide pupils with a list of near-obsolete nouns, and ask them to suggest which modern words have replaced them and why. Examples could include 'bedpan', 'breeches', 'telegram' and 'carriage'. See if they can identify some specific contexts in which we still use these words.

Location, Location, Location

10

Extra Background

A dialect is a regional manner of speech. Accent refers to the pronunciation of words, which may differ from region to region, e.g. how 'bath' is said with a long or short 'a' sound.

Extension Idea

Ask pupils to research the different words used for 'bun' — there are lots of different variants, such as: 'barm cake', 'bap', 'bread roll', 'batch', 'muffin', 'cob'.

Extension Idea

Collect the pupils' answers and encourage them to add them to a map of the country. They could then add examples of words, phrases, or even real/fictional people for each dialect.

Location, Location, Location

Different places in Britain (and across the world) have their own varieties of English, called dialects. As well as using different pronunciations of words (this is called 'accent'), dialects often use some different words altogether.

Which word do you use for these?

Hint: These aren't "trainers" — they're what you'd wear for gym indoors.

I call these ✏ pumps

Did you know that people in different parts of the UK have completely different words for these? In the south-east of England they're often called 'plimsolls', in the north-west they're called 'pumps', in the south-west they're called 'daps', and in some parts of Scotland they're called 'sand shoes'.

Can you think of any other objects which have different names in different parts of the country? Write the objects and their different names in the box below.

How about words for 'sandwich' or 'child'?

> ✏ I know that in some places people call a child a 'bairn'. Sandwiches can be called 'baps' or 'butties'. My uncle in London says 'barnet' instead of 'hair'.

Can you name any dialects in Britain, and where they're from?

E.g. 'Scouse' is from Liverpool.

The dialect in London is called Cockney.
The dialect in Newcastle is called Geordie

Different varieties of English are spoken across the world. Do you know any words they say in other English-speaking countries (like Australia, South Africa, America, India or Pakistan) that we don't say in Britain? Write them below.

> ✏ A South African word for 'trainers' is 'takkies'. In Australia they are called 'joggers'.

For example, in America they say "sidewalk" for 'pavement'. In Australia they say "fair dinkum" for 'true'.

Section 1 — Change And Exchange

© CGP — not to be photocopied

Extra Background

Until the first half of the 20th century, having a strong dialect and accent were often stigmatised as markers of a lack of wealth. It was common for less educated people to speak the dialect and accent of their region, and for educated people to speak in 'Received Pronunciation', using 'Standard' English.

Location, Location, Location — Aims:

- to investigate regional variations in English, both across the UK and globally
- to consider the point at which a dialect becomes a new language, in order to explore how languages are related and defined.

Some dialects are almost <u>unintelligible</u> to many other English speakers. Have a look at this sentence from the Isle of Man.

> There's a scutch o' snigs in the baie by the broogh.

This means 'there's a lot of sand-eels in the bay by the headland'.

Unintelligible means un-understandable!

The example below is from Hawaiian English. Can you work out what it means?

"Get tu mach turis naudeiz."

I think it means: ✎ 'we have too much tourism nowadays'

Is this still English, even if you can't understand it? Explain your answer.

How difficult to understand do you think a dialect needs to be before it becomes a completely different language?

✎ I think that if only the speakers of a dialect can understand it, then it should become a different language.

Who do you think decides when a dialect becomes a different language?

As we've seen, sometimes speakers can struggle to understand <u>different varieties</u> of their own language. On the other hand, sometimes people who speak <u>different languages</u> can actually understand each other! For example, many speakers in Norway and Sweden can understand each other's speech, even though Norwegian and Swedish are different languages.

The linguist Max Weinreich said: "A language is a dialect with an army and a navy." What do you think he meant by this?

A linguist is someone who studies languages.

✎ I think he meant that when you have an army and navy you can take a country over, and then your 'dialect' can become the language of that place.

Do you think it's a good or a bad thing that English has lots of dialects?

✎ I think it's a good thing because it makes our language more interesting.

Section 1 — Change And Exchange

Suggested Scaffolding

Ask pupils if any of the words look similar to those they know, and encourage them to try different pronunciations of words like 'naudeiz'.

Pupil Guidance

Pupils who answer 'yes' may explain that these are still 'English' words, just with different spellings to reflect pronunciation. Pupils who answer 'no' may explain that these words are unrecognisable to them, so this isn't English any more.

Pupil Guidance

Pupils might say 'the people who write the dictionaries' or 'the government'.

Suggested Scaffolding

Children may need to revisit the idea of language families to understand how some languages can be very similar. You may need to ask them what an army and navy can do, and prompt them to think about what happened to languages in history when one country conquered another, or people migrated to a country.

Pupil Guidance

Pupils may also suggest that it would be better if everyone spoke in the same way so that everyone could understand each other, but get pupils to consider whether this would lead to the loss of interesting words and/or ideas.

Your Own Language

Extra Background

Idiolect is derived from the Greek word 'idios' (one's own), and the root 'lect', meaning speech. In Ancient Greece, an 'idiot', was someone who was only concerned with their own affairs.

Suggested Scaffolding

If pupils struggle, ask them to think about some of their favourite book, film or TV characters and whether they have any catch phrases. For example, if they watch 'The Simpsons ™' they might recognise that Homer says 'D'oh!', 'Woo-hoo!' or 'Why you little...!' a lot.

Pupil Guidance

Idiolect is not just about dialect, accent, the language you speak or where you come from. It is about how you personally choose and use words.

---

12   **Section 2 — Register**

Idiolect

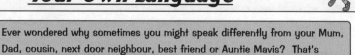

Your Own Language

Ever wondered why sometimes you might speak differently from your Mum, Dad, cousin, next door neighbour, best friend or Auntie Mavis? That's because you have your own idiolect — the language you personally use.

Your dialect is how you speak based on where you live and your idiolect is your very own, unique language. So even though we speak in a certain dialect, our language can still be different from that of our friends and family.

Your idiolect is a bit like your fingerprint — no one else speaks exactly the same as you do!

You might talk a bit differently from your friend.

"Well, she was, like, I want, like, that t-shirt, like."

"That's great! Yes please! That's great!"

You could use the word 'like' a lot...   ... but your friend might say 'that's great' a lot.

Think about the words and phrases of your own idiolect. Are there any words or phrases that you're particularly fond of saying?

✏ I say 'right' and 'OK' a lot, and my friend says 'like' all the time in between words. Another of my friends says 'yanno?' (you know) a lot.

Have a think about someone else's idiolect. Choose somebody else and write down what you notice about the words and phrases they tend to use.

✏ My granny says "That's spiffing" a lot. I think that's because she's a bit older.

Why do you think you and that person speak differently?

Pupil Guidance

Answers might include references to age, nationality, interests etc.

Your Own Language — Aims:

- to understand what idiolect is, and to investigate how we each develop one
- to reflect on the influences on our own idiolect, and whether it is subject to change
- to consider how our idiolect may be perceived by others when it differs from theirs.

Some of the things that make up your idiolect can be determined by where you live, who you live with, or even by the television programmes you watch, and books you read.

Where do you think your own idiolect has come from?

Are you influenced by any other cultures and their language?

✎ I grew up with some of it, because my family taught it to me. I think I picked up some from my friends and people at school, and maybe a bit more from things I watch on TV.

Look at this example below. Liam has just won the lottery. Jago and Elaine have commented on his win.

"Back of the net! What a result!"

⬅ Jago

Liam

"That's put the icing on the cake for you!"

Elaine ⟹

What do you notice about the way Jago and Elaine have commented on Liam's win?

✎ Jago is using language from sport — probably because he likes sport. Elaine is using language to do with baking.

Your idiolect can also change over time. Think about what new words and phrases you've learnt this year. Write them down here.

Selfie (a photograph of yourself), idiolect (the language you use)

Why do you think you've changed the way you speak?

How and why might your language change in the future?

✎ My language may change when I change school, or if I learn something from a TV show or something new at school.

Extra Background

Some pupils' idiolects might contain jargon (words associated with a particular group). For example, if they go to Guides or Scouts they might use words like 'Sixer', 'pack' and 'taps'.

Extension Idea

Ask pupils to think about words they use because they hear them on TV. Get them to write down any examples.

Suggested Scaffolding

Pupils might think about whether they have taken up a new hobby or sport this year, and what words they have learnt from that.

Pupil Guidance

Being consciously aware of idiolect means that we can vary it. We can change what we say, and how we say it, to fit in with, or be understood by, the people to whom we are talking.

Pupil Guidance

One of the biggest reasons for someone's idiolect changing is social change. Children should consider how they might move in the future — classes at school, friendship groups, town etc.

Speaking A Bit Differently

14

Extra Background

'Code-switching' can be used to describe when a speaker alters their register to make it more appropriate for the situation — just as Mary does in the passage on page 14.

Pupil Guidance

We often change register subtly when we are with different friends. We can mirror their turns of phrase, or use words they use, to reinforce our friendship with them.

Pupil Guidance

The author uses Mary's willingness to code-switch to show that she has a close relationship with Dickon.

Extension Idea

Ask students to have a go at speaking in different dialects. They could choose from Yorkshire, Scottish, Cockney, or even further abroad, e.g. American or Australian.

Speaking A Bit Differently

 Do you speak the same way all the time? Have you ever tried to change the way you talk to fit in with where you are and who you're with? Lots of people do it all the time...

Look at this passage from 'The Secret Garden' by Frances Hodgson Burnett. It is about a girl called Mary who speaks Standard English. Here she has chosen to speak with a Yorkshire dialect to a boy called Dickon.

'Standard English' is a form of English that doesn't contain any dialect words.

... *"Aye, that we mun,"* she said (which meant *"Yes, indeed, we must").* *"I'll tell thee what us'll do first,"* she proceeded, and Dickon grinned, because when the little *wench* tried to twist her tongue into speaking Yorkshire it amused him very much...

...When she stopped she was quite proud of herself. She had never made a long speech in Yorkshire before and she had remembered very well.

wench = girl   *F Hodgson Burnett 'The Secret Garden' (1911)*

Write down an example of where Mary is speaking in a Yorkshire dialect.

✏ 'Aye, that we mun', and 'I'll tell thee what us'll do first' are both examples of Mary speaking in 'Yorkshire'.

Why do you think Mary changed the way she spoke?

✏ I think that Mary wanted to speak like Dickon for fun, and because she is his friend and wants to be more like him.

Look at how Dickon reacts to her efforts to speak in a Yorkshire dialect. Do you think she's been successful? Explain your answer.

✏ Dickon grins, so I think she's been successful in amusing him, but Dickon's amusement suggests that she hasn't been very successful in speaking with a Yorkshire accent.

 When do we try to copy how other people speak? And when do we not?

Pupil Guidance

Pupils may be aware of occasions when they feel the need to use particular words from a dialect other than their own in order to integrate with an existing group. They may suggest that they might not copy the way others speak when they're comfortable that they can understand each other.

Speaking A Bit Differently — Aims:

- to investigate the ways in which register differs when we speak to different people
- to consider how and why registers we use might be more or less formal
- to enable pupils to be consciously aware of their different registers and how they use them.

15

Sometimes the way you speak depends on where you are or who you're with. Some situations are more <u>formal</u> than others. If something is formal, it means you're expected to act in a serious and respectful way.

Look at these situations below. Do you think they're informal or formal? Put them in the right columns, then add one of your own for each category.

having lunch at school

a wedding

shopping with friends

a funeral

a friend's birthday party

Grandma's birthday party

Informal	Formal
Lunch at school, shopping with friends, a friend's birthday party.	A wedding or a funeral, or Grandma's birthday party.

Are any of your answers different to a friend's? Why might this be?

The more formal the situation and occasion, the more formal your spoken register would be.

Here are some phrases you might hear in an informal situation. How might you change them in a more formal situation?

"Coming through — move out the way!"

'Excuse me, please, could you let me pass?'

Your register is <u>how</u> you speak in a certain situation.

"Hey Bob, can I have the gravy?"

'Robert, please could you pass me the gravy? Thank you.'

How might you say the following sentence in an informal way?

"Would you mind if I telephoned you this afternoon?"

'Can I give you a ring this afternoon?'

Describe an example of when you changed the way you spoke because of where you were.

When I was being told off by my teacher, I had to try and remember to speak more politely, so she didn't get cross.

Extra Background
'Register' is a particular style of language used for a particular type of social interaction. Register can be informal or formal.

Pupil Guidance
Some students may think 'Grandma's party' or 'a wedding' are informal situations, which opens up the discussion about how relationships can influence register.

Extension Idea
Pupils could role-play each of these situations, and record the language they use. Get them to see to what extent they are code-switching unconsciously already.

Suggested Scaffolding
Children who struggle with this concept may benefit from a role-play where the informal and formal registers are said by different characters.

Extension Idea
Get students to write an etiquette book. It could be filled with examples of when to use a particular register.

Active Or Passive?

Extra Background

Pupils may not be aware of it, but they all use the passive voice — often for avoiding responsibility!

'Mrs Jones, the glass vase has been broken!'

'Well, who broke it?'

'I don't know, it just got broken...'

When pupils understand that there is a mysterious agent who broke the vase, it's quite easy for them to understand the concept.

Pupil Guidance

The auxiliary verb 'was' is used with the past participle of the verb to form the past tense. Pupils need to be sure they don't confuse this with the past progressive tense, e.g. 'I was looking.'

Pupil Guidance

Children should be able to recognise that they generally use the active voice.

Suggested Scaffolding

Write out what happened in the active voice first, and then turn it into the passive sentence by sentence.

16

Active Or Passive?

You might not even realise it, but most of the time, you're probably using the <u>active voice</u> to describe things happening. But if you jumble up the order and add in a couple of words, you can talk in the <u>passive voice</u>. How clever!

In the <u>active voice</u>, the subject does something to the object.

> George tidied the kitchen.

In the <u>passive voice</u>, something is done to the subject by the object.

> The kitchen was tidied by George.

Can you write out these sentences using the passive voice?

Jane visited the castle. The castle was .... visited .... by ...... Jane ......

Moonlight flooded the road. ➡ The road was flooded by moonlight.

A wave overwhelmed the ship. ➡ The ship was overwhelmed by a wave.

Write down a sentence of your own in the passive voice.

The beach was polluted by the oil spill from the shipwreck.

Do you generally use the active or passive voice when speaking?

The passive voice is often used in police reports. Can you write a summary of a crime scene in the speech bubble below? Be as creative as you can!

'At 4.30 pm, reports were received that Stomper's Shoe factory had been burgled. Size 15 footprints were found at the scene of the crime, and a window to the rear of the property was smashed. Several boxes of shoes were stolen. A false moustache was found nearby, so it is believed a disguise was used.

Why do you think police reports often use the passive voice?

Section 2 — Register

© CGP — not to be photocopied

Pupil Guidance

Using the passive voice avoids mentioning a subject, which makes the report more impersonal. Police officers often have to describe what's happened without knowing who did it.

Active Or Passive? — Aims:

- to investigate register in the context of using active or passive voice
- to consider the functions and usages of passive voice texts and to identify their purpose
- to enable pupils to practise writing in the passive voice and consider its effects.

The passive voice can be impersonal. <u>Impersonal language</u> is when you don't refer to the thing, person or agent doing the action.

The kitchen was tidied by George. ← This is the <u>passive voice</u>.

The kitchen was tidied. ← This is <u>impersonal</u>.

Tick the box next to the sentence which uses impersonal language. Rewrite the one you didn't tick using impersonal language.

[ ] *"I washed all the dishes."*

[✓] *"It can be argued that English is fun."*

All the dishes were washed.

The passive voice is usually used to write scientific reports. Why do you think this is?

Here's an experiment write-up. Can you rewrite it using impersonal language?

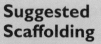

Impersonal language often uses the passive voice.

Yasmin and I poured the muddy water through a filter which we'd made. Then we waited for it to filter through. I poured the clean water into a flask and then heated it until it boiled. Finally, Yasmin mixed food dye into the clean water which she knew would turn it green.

✎ The muddy water was poured through a home-made filter. When it had filtered through, the clean water was poured into a flask and heated until it boiled. Food dye was then mixed into the clean water in order to turn it green.

What effect does using the passive voice have on your writing?

✎ The passive voice makes writing much more impersonal, more formal and sometimes less friendly.

Suggested Scaffolding

Use this as an example: 'The boy kicked the football.' (active). 'The football was kicked by the boy.' (passive). 'The football was kicked.' (impersonal). Model sentences like this.

Extra Background

The passive voice makes writing less personal, particularly scientific reports. It focuses the reader's attention on <u>what</u> has been done rather than <u>who</u> has done it.

Extension Idea

Ask pupils to work in pairs. One pupil should tell the other how they did something, for example, built a model plane, made a den, painted a picture. The pupil that is listening should write down what their partner says and then rewrite it — once as a set of instructions using verbs in the imperative, and once in the passive voice as if it were an experiment write-up.

Extension Idea

Ask pupils why the passive voice might not be appropriate for fiction. One reason is that it slows down the pace and makes the action less immediate and dramatic.

Becoming More Formal

18

Becoming More Formal

 There are lots of features of good formal English that you can use in your writing. But as we'll see later, it's important not to go over the top...

This (made-up) radio broadcast is written in formal English. Underline any words or phrases in the broadcast that make it sound formal.

Look up any words you don't know in the dictionary.

"_Reports have emerged_ of a spaceship landing in the Forest of Dean, and _of the abduction_ of several locals. _It is not yet known_ how many people are involved. There have been _numerous sightings_ of extraterrestrials in the local area, with at least four shopkeepers _currently being treated_ for shock."

The broadcast uses the passive voice, such as "It is not yet known..." rather than "We don't yet know...". What effect does this have? Circle all the answers that apply.

It makes it less personal.

It makes it more formal.

It sounds more trustworthy.

It makes it more informal.

It's easier to listen to.

Now read the follow-up to the broadcast...

Now for an update on the Gloucestershire space invasion. The extraterrestrials have demanded that a ransom of twenty thousand parsnips be paid within the next 2 hours. The Prime Minister is reported to have agreed to this request, on the strict condition that the spaceship leave the Solar System immediately thereafter. He has ordered that the spaceship be given parsnips only, and no carrots, or he'll "get a bit cross".

There are examples here of the subjunctive mood: "that a ransom... be paid", "that the spaceship leave". This is a characteristic of formal language.

Copy out another example of the subjunctive mood from the passage.

'He has ordered that the spaceship be given'

Section 2 — Register

© CGP — not to be photocopied

Becoming More Formal — Aims:

- to investigate the characteristics of formal and informal writing
- to consider the purposes and types of formal writing, and how formal writing can be abused
- to consider what makes good, effective formal writing.

Can you put these words on a scale to show how formal they are?

✏ ~~verbalise~~   natter   chat   communicate   ~~talk~~

less formal ...natter.... chat.... talk communicate verbalise... more formal

As you can see from the broadcasts, formal English often uses more long words than normal spoken English. However, good formal English still needs to be polite, plain and easy to understand.

The writer of this letter has tried to use formal English, but they've gone too far. Rewrite it using English that's still formal, but plainer and easier to understand.

Dear Sir,

   I write to inform you of the situation regarding your tall, flowering vegetation which is currently overshadowing my garden. The plants' excessive growth continually inconveniences my household, depriving us of sunlight for the greater part of the day.

   Kindly ensure that the offending plants be suitably decreased in size. If this request is not met, I am afraid we shall have to take matters — and a saw — into our own hands.

Yours faithfully,

Mr O. T. Thompson (no. 34)

Dear Neighbour,
✏ I'm sorry to bother you, but I believe you may not have noticed how tall your plants have grown recently. They don't cast a shadow over you, but they do over us, and we are finding that they block out a lot of sunlight.
Could you possibly do something about reducing their height? If you aren't able to cut them, perhaps we could do this for you?
Thank you.
Yours faithfully,
Olly Thompson.

What makes good, effective formal language?

✏ Good, effective formal language is polite, clear and easy to understand.

Extra Background

Formal English is fine, but over-formal English can sometimes sound over the top. It can give the impression that the writer is trying to sound superior to the person they are writing to.

Extension Idea

Get students to read the letter and think about their reaction. Ask them if it would make them want to do what the writer has asked, or if it would have the opposite effect.

Suggested Scaffolding

Suggest that pupils put down in plain English what they want the neighbour to do, then write it out in formal, polite sentences.

Pupil Guidance

Letters beginning 'Dear Sir/Madam', have 'yours faithfully' as a closing phrase. Letters addressed to a specific person end with 'yours sincerely'. Letters beginning 'Dear Jess' usually take less formal endings such as 'love' or 'best wishes'.

Red, Amber Or Green?

20   *Section 3 — Word Art*

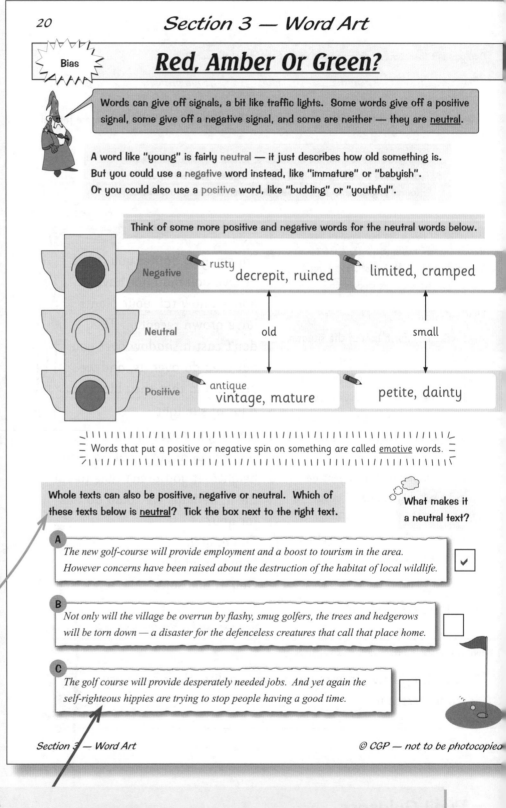

Red, Amber Or Green?

Bias

Words can give off signals, a bit like traffic lights. Some words give off a positive signal, some give off a negative signal, and some are neither — they are <u>neutral</u>.

A word like "young" is fairly neutral — it just describes how old something is.
But you could use a negative word instead, like "immature" or "babyish".
Or you could also use a positive word, like "budding" or "youthful".

Think of some more positive and negative words for the neutral words below.

Negative	rusty decrepit, ruined	limited, cramped
Neutral	old	small
Positive	antique vintage, mature	petite, dainty

Words that put a positive or negative spin on something are called <u>emotive</u> words.

Whole texts can also be positive, negative or neutral. Which of these texts below is <u>neutral</u>? Tick the box next to the right text.

What makes it a neutral text?

A *The new golf-course will provide employment and a boost to tourism in the area. However concerns have been raised about the destruction of the habitat of local wildlife.* ✓

B *Not only will the village be overrun by flashy, smug golfers, the trees and hedgerows will be torn down — a disaster for the defenceless creatures that call that place home.* ☐

C *The golf course will provide desperately needed jobs. And yet again the self-righteous hippies are trying to stop people having a good time.* ☐

Extra Background

Biased language is used to present a point of view, and to 'spin' or influence the reader's perception of a situation. The writer's choice of positive or negative words can indicate their opinion, and the opinion they want their reader to adopt.

Extension Idea

Get students to write a full letter using one of these points of view. Perhaps they want the golf course built because their parents/carers could work there. Or maybe they don't want it built because it will cause lots of construction noise at school. Ask them to write a letter using the most biased and emotive language they can. Read the letters out loud and see if anyone is persuaded.

Pupil Guidance

Generalisations are often a feature of emotive, biased writing, e.g. "children don't get enough exercise" makes it sound as though lack of exercise is an issue affecting <u>all</u> children.

Red, Amber Or Green? — Aims:

- to allow pupils to investigate the concept of biased language, and how and why it might be used
- to get pupils to consider how biased language is specifically designed to influence its reader
- to enable pupils to identify when a text might be biased, and to be aware that writers might try to influence them using biased language.

21

When a text presents something in an overly positive or negative light, we say it is <u>biased</u>. Choose one of the texts from page 20 which is biased. Circle whether it is biased <u>in favour of</u> or <u>against</u> the golf course. Then write down the <u>emotive</u> words and phrases it uses below.

Text __B__ is biased in favour of / (against) the golf course.

✎ It uses words such as 'overrun', 'flashy', 'smug', 'torn down', 'disaster', 'defenceless' and 'home'.

Bias usually depends on <u>who</u> is talking or writing. Who do you think may have written the biased texts? Think about why they might be strongly for or against the golf course.

Text __B__ may have been written by _a wildlife charity._
Text __C__ may have been written by _a person who needs a job._

Being outrageously biased can be quite fun! Think of an event you've been to recently — maybe a concert, a sports match or a school trip. Write a couple of sentences to describe it — first with very positive bias, then with negative bias.

> Remember to use plenty of emotive words.

The museum was brought to life by a lively bunch of busy school children, who chatted amongst themselves and shared their sweets happily.

The whole experience of the museum was ruined by a group of youths, who screamed like banshees and guzzled hundreds of sweets.

Any words we hear or read might be biased in some way. What should you bear in mind when you're listening to people, or reading what they have written? Write down your thoughts below.

✎ You should bear in mind what speakers/writers might want you to do or think, and watch out for emotive language that might be biased.

What does it mean when we say that a text is biased?

✎ A text is biased when it uses emotive language to present a point of view that the writer wants you to agree with.

Section 3 — Word Art

Pupil Guidance

Pupils may answer that 'C' is in favour of the golf course, and uses words and phrases like 'desperately', 'yet again' and 'self-righteous'.

Extra Background

Propaganda and spin are used frequently during election campaigns.

Suggested Scaffolding

Read the sample answers to the pupils. Do they think that the pupils are behaving differently in each text, or is it the perception of the writer that is different?

Pupil Guidance

Bias exists whenever anyone wants to change your mind. Pupils could be asked if they're aware of bias in the media, e.g. the portrayals of celebrities on television or in magazines. Ask them why they have to be careful with these sources.

Extension Idea

Ask pupils to bring in examples of biased language that they come across outside school. Ask them to explain how they spotted it to you/other pupils.

Attractive Advertising

Extra Background

Alliteration and rhyme are used in adverts to catch the customer's eye and make slogans more memorable. Imperatives are used frequently in adverts to speak directly to the customer.

Pupil Guidance

Lists of three are another persuasive technique. They're covered in more detail on page 27.

Suggested Scaffolding

Some students might need a thesaurus or a rhyming dictionary to help them with this task.

Pupil Guidance

Rhetorical questions rely on the writer accurately judging the reader's feelings about something (i.e. that they *are* stuck in a routine). In adverts, they often draw attention to negatives, in order to offer more attractive solutions (here, a holiday).

22

Writing to persuade

Attractive Advertising

There are lots of special tricks advertisers use to entice and excite us. Let's have a look at some important examples...

1 Adverts often start with a <u>catchy slogan</u> that sticks in your head.

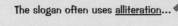 Bahamas Beach — bathe in the blissful blue!   Bahamas Bay — just a day away!

The slogan often uses <u>alliteration</u>...   ...or <u>rhyme</u>.

2 Adverts can also use <u>imperative verbs</u> to tell you to do something.

VISIT the museums. EXPLORE the caves. ENJOY the beaches.

Write two different sentences to advertise a brand of orange juice. Write one as a catchy slogan using alliteration or rhyme, and the other using three imperative verbs.

✎ A tasty drink that's delicious and nutritious.
Drink Olga's Orange Juice — taste the flavour, enjoy the zest.

3 Adverts also use <u>rhetorical questions</u> — questions that you're not actually supposed to answer, or that only have one reasonable answer.

Look at this text below. Underline all the rhetorical questions.

<u>Stuck in the same old routine?</u> <u>Bored of waking up to rain and drizzle?</u>
Well now's your chance to take a holiday! <u>But how about a holiday with a twist?</u>

With CGP Travel, we guarantee you'll see the world through different eyes.
Sample exotic food, experience fantastical adventures and feel the sun on your skin.

<u>So what are you waiting for?</u>

Now choose two of the rhetorical questions from above.
Write them down, then explain the effect they have on the reader.

Try to think of more than 'it makes you want to go on holiday'.

Rhetorical question: ✎ 'Stuck in the same old routine?'
Effect: This makes you question whether you are leading a boring life.
Rhetorical question: 'Bored of waking up to rain and drizzle?'
Effect: This makes you think it would be great to be somewhere sunny.

Attractive Advertising — Aims:

- to consider the nature and function of persuasive language
- to investigate some of the specific linguistic features used in advertising
- to enable pupils to practise using persuasive language in a specific context by writing adverts.

4 Adverts sometimes use <u>word play</u>, like puns and jokes.

It would be a missed steak not to eat here!

This would be a good <u>pun</u> for a restaurant advert (missed steak = mistake).

Carrion is what vultures eat, but it's a pun because it sounds like 'carry on'.

Vulture Airlines — free carrion luggage!

Think of some words to do with these products.

a climbing holiday → ropes   rocks   hook   going up   helmet   grip   boulder

a brand of honey → hive   bees   sweet   buzz   bcekeeper   honeycomb   sting

hairdressing business → snip   cut   scissors   curl   barber   dry   wash

Now choose one product from above and use word play to write a sentence advertising it.

Get a grip — choose Clifton's Climbing Holidays!

Think of a product — something you would really like yourself, and write the text for a radio advert. Try to include a catchy slogan, imperative verbs, rhetorical questions and word play.

Weary of wet, weak video games? Does life drag on? Then you need Dragon Deep! Enjoy the excitement as elegant elves and high-powered heroes chase the dark dragon, Dina, through terrible terrains. Slay the serpent, find the jewels of Jarod and return triumphant to the Tall Tower. Want the greatest game ever? Then buy now and get ahead. Dragon Deep — a monster of a video game!

Which techniques are often used to create effective adverts?

Slogans, imperative verbs, rhetorical questions and puns.

Extra Background

Puns are phrases which have two different, but often related, meanings, and they can come in different forms. Some puns use homophones e.g. 'bolder' / 'boulder', some use homographs e.g. 'buzz', (the sound made by bees / a feeling of excitement). Other puns rely on rhyme, e.g. 'boys and curls' (rather than 'boys and girls').

Suggested Scaffolding

If pupils are struggling, give them a suitable word, and ask them to think about whether the word has more than one meaning. Suitable words might be: 'rock' for the climbing holiday ('a boulder' / 'That rocks!'); 'buzz' for the honey ('the sound that bees make' / 'a thrill') and 'snip' for the hairdressing business ('to cut' / 'a bargain').

Extension Idea

Get pupils to do this in groups, creating an advert for, e.g. a video game. They can present to the class and see who would buy it by a show of hands. Discuss what the winning advert does well.

Pupil Guidance

Not every advert will use all of these techniques — encourage pupils to try different combinations to see what is most effective.

Time For An Argument

Writing to argue

Time For An Argument

It's really important to be able to construct a convincing argument... it means you can bring people round to your way of thinking!

Read these two arguments. Both are in favour of having more PE lessons per week.

A

"We should definitely have more PE at school. Everyone really loves it, especially me. I play netball twice a week outside school. I'd like to be able to show how good I am to everyone else in school. Also, some people are really lazy, so they need to be more active. I'm not lazy at all — the opposite in fact. I walk to and from school almost every day, except on Thursdays when my mum drives me in. Everyone definitely wants more PE at school. We should have at least 3 hours a week. Anyone who disagrees is just saying that because they're no good at sport."

B

"There are lots of subjects which would benefit from more lesson time. Maths and English lessons, for example, teach us skills we will need in the future. Also, many of us in the class would enjoy more time spent learning about history and geography.

However, PE is important not only to our learning, but also to our health and well-being. Some of us don't do much sport outside of school, so PE lessons are vital for us to keep fit. In addition, the team games we do in PE teach us valuable skills in leadership and working as a team. These are important social skills that can be used in other areas.

Furthermore, most other local schools already have more PE lessons per week than we do.

So in conclusion I believe that one extra hour per week spent on PE would be reasonable."

Let's have a think about some of the features of language in these two arguments. Write down whether each of these is a feature of argument A or B.

A .... *uses the words "I", "me" or "my" repeatedly.*
B .... *uses examples of other schools.*
A .... *uses the word "definitely" twice.*
A .... *criticises other people.*
A .... *uses the words "everyone" and "anyone".*
B .... *considers other points of view.*
B .... *uses connectives like "however", "in addition" and "furthermore".*
B .... *is split into paragraphs.*

Why might these language features make the arguments better or worse? Discuss your ideas with a friend.

Extra Background

Argument texts and persuasive texts share a lot of features, e.g. rhetorical questions and emotive language, but they do have differences. Argument texts are often more balanced and think about alternative view-points.

Pupil Guidance

An overly-personal point of view (like this one) is often not effective.

Suggested Scaffolding

When writing their own argument texts, pupils can be encouraged to leave out the things in this list labelled 'A', and include the things on this list labelled 'B'.

Pupil Guidance

The features of text 'B' make the argument well structured and balanced. The features of text 'A' make the text one-sided and personal.

Time For An Argument — Aims:

- to consider the functions of argument texts, and investigate their specific features
- to investigate what makes an argument text effective and how words can be used to demonstrate a point of view or persuade
- to create an argument text with appropriate features.

Which argument do you think is more convincing, and why? Fill in the boxes below.

I think argument **B** .... is more convincing than argument **A** ....

Reasons why this argument is good:

It is balanced, and considers other points of view. It makes reasonable points, and it uses persuasive arguments about health. It is well structured and uses connectives.

Reasons why this argument is bad:

It is too personal and biased. It's repetitive and has a bad structure. It doesn't look at other points of view. It uses generalisations like 'everyone'. It gives opinions without any reasons to back them up.

It's time for you to construct your own argument. Write to your headteacher arguing for a change in school life. Maybe you want a school trip somewhere? Or maybe you'd prefer not to wear a school uniform? Ask for whatever you want... just make your argument convincing!

> Make sure your argument is balanced. Think of the arguments 'against', as well as the arguments 'for'.

Some people might say that building a new playground would be too expensive, but there are also many benefits.
Children need to play and get exercise, and our current playground is too small to do this. If we built a new playground, it would be enjoyed by generations of children.
In addition, it would also create jobs for local builders, so it's not just children who would benefit.

How will you use what you've learnt on these pages to make your arguments more effective?

I will think about the other side of the argument, and use connectives to make sure my text is well structured.

Extra Background

Writing, listening to, and reading aloud argument texts can help pupils understand what makes an argument effective. Subjects for debate can be drawn from Science, History and Geography, not just literacy lessons.

Suggested Scaffolding

Pupils can discuss the subject of their argument text with an adult or friend, and then make notes about the points they'd like to include. They could then cut out each point separately and shuffle them into an order they're happy with.

Pupil Guidance

Discourse markers such as 'in addition' and generalisations such as 'some people might say' are often used to signal a change of point in argument texts. Pupils may find a list of discourse markers helpful.

Pupil Guidance

Pupils should be able to mention specific features of argument texts.

7/9/15

Now, Repeat After Me...

26

Extra Background

Repetition, like rhyme, alliteration and the use of rhetorical questions, can be used to persuade. It can be used in adverts, in argument texts, and is particularly effective in texts for public speaking.

Extension Idea

Get pupils to research and/or listen to Winston Churchill's speeches. You could then look at some wartime propaganda posters, and see if pupils can spot any similarities in the ways in which they persuade people to support the war effort.

Pupil Guidance

These speeches use first and second person pronouns (e.g. "we" and "you") to appeal directly to the listeners.

Repetition

Now, Repeat After Me...

Repeating words or phrases can make your writing more persuasive. It can help show how passionately you feel about something.

Here is an extract from a speech by Winston Churchill, the Prime Minister of Great Britain during the Second World War. Circle the words or phrases that he repeats.

'We shall go on to the end. We shall fight in France, we shall fight on the seas and oceans, we shall fight with growing confidence and growing strength in the air, we shall defend our island, whatever the cost may be. We shall fight on the beaches, we shall fight on the landing grounds, we shall fight in the fields and in the streets, we shall fight in the hills; we shall never surrender..."

Winston Churchill, given in the House of Commons, 4th June 1940

Imagine you were listening to this speech in wartime. How would it make you feel?

I would be worried about the war, but I would realise that the Prime Minister thought that if we kept fighting, we would win.

Based on this speech, what kind of man do you think Winston Churchill was? Write down three adjectives that you think describe his character.

determined, inspirational and brave

This next example is by John F. Kennedy, President of the United States of America from 1961 to 1963. He repeats words and phrases, but also the <u>structure</u> of the second sentence is almost a repetition of the first.

"And so, my fellow Americans: ask not what your country can do for you; ask what you can do for your country. My fellow citizens of the world: ask not what America will do for you, but what together we can do for the freedom of man."

John F. Kennedy, Inaugural address, 20th January 1961

Have a go at reading this aloud. Think about how the structure of the sentences affects the way you read it.

Section 3 — Word Art

© CGP — not to be photocopied

Pupil Guidance

The punctuation in this speech makes you pause in the right place, so that 'ask not what' and 'ask what' are emphasised further.

Now, Repeat After Me... — Aims:

- to allow pupils to consider repetition as a persuasive technique
- to demonstrate to pupils how texts can be made persuasive by selective emphasis and lists of three
- to enable pupils to practise creating a persuasive text using repetition, emphasis and a list of three.

A useful persuasive technique is to state things in a <u>list of three</u>. Here is an example by another US President — Franklin D Roosevelt.

*"This great Nation **will endure** as it has endured, **will revive** and **will prosper**."*

Franklin D Roosevelt First Inaugural address, 4th March 1933

The 'list of three' technique isn't just used in English. The motto for the French Republic is "Liberté, Égalité, Fraternité" ("Freedom, Equality, Brotherhood").

Think of a list of three as a motto for your school.

It doesn't have to be too serious. Lists of three can be amusing too!

 " Friendship , Laughter , Learning "

Imagine your school is being threatened with closure — the council wants to sell the land to make way for a supermarket. You have to make a speech to your classmates to persuade them to go on a protest march to save your school.

First think of some words or phrases that you're going to repeat, and a list of three if you can.

strength, safety, stability; we need; knowledge; learning; wisdom; sharing; friendship

Now write your full speech here.

 We, the children of this school, need a place of learning. We need a place to develop our knowledge, wisdom and our friendships. We need a place to call our own. This school is a place of sharing, it is a place of strength, safety and stability. To demolish it would be selfish, cruel and wrong.

How can repeating words and phrases make your writing more persuasive?

Repetition makes your point clearer and easier to remember. You can also combine it with lists of three.

Section 3 — Word Art

Extra Background

The speeches on these pages were written to be spoken and remembered, not to be read. They use techniques that combine persuasion with poetry.

Extension Idea

Challenge pupils to use alliteration or rhyme when creating their lists of three.

Suggested Scaffolding

Start by encouraging pupils to write down all the points they want to make about why their school shouldn't close. Then see if any of these can be grouped together into lists of three, or perhaps alliterative pairs. Get them to think about which phrases would be best to repeat (e.g. emotive ones such as 'we need').

Pupil Guidance

Remind pupils not to overuse repetition — it can lose its effectiveness if it is used too frequently.

Feeling A Little Moody

Extra Background

The weather can strongly influence the mood of a story. Writers often use personification to make a setting more emotive, e.g. 'the thunder muttered aggressively'.

Pupil Guidance

Verbs can add pace and excitement because they provide a sense of movement. Adjectives can provide finer details.

Pupil Guidance

Pupils might circle 'screeching' and 'swerving' as verbs, but they're actually being used as adjectives in this example.

Extension Idea

Get pupils to try using these techniques themselves. Write some passages with lots of verbs but few adjectives, and vice versa, and ask them to discuss the mood that has been created.

28

 Mood

Feeling A Little Moody

 What happens when you read a ghost story? Do you get scared? That probably means the writer has done a good job in setting the mood. Let's have a look at how you can set the mood in your writing.

Look at the passage below. Think about the words the writer uses. How do they make you feel?

The weather had been fine all day, but as they approached the castle the clouds began to gather, and the trees creaked and groaned with the swelling wind. The setting sun had cast huge shadows over the lawns, and ravens complained bitterly overhead.

I feel as if something bad is about to happen. It feels like there might soon be something dangerous or scary.

If there are lots of <u>verbs</u> in a passage, the mood tends to be quite different from a passage that is full of <u>adjectives</u>. Can you think why this would be?

Here's a text with lots of verbs. Circle all the verbs in the passage.

And all of a sudden, they (were) free, (running) through the streets. They (felt) like if they (went) any faster they (would fly). They (skipped) and (danced) around all the statue-like people; (waltzed) and (pirouetted) their way through the screeching cars and swerving bikes.

What mood does the author create by using the dramatic verbs above?

Dramatic verbs help you to picture what is happening and, in this case, to know exactly how the characters are moving.

Now read this text with lots of adjectives instead. How would you describe the mood?

The lion's large, dark eyes rested on the hazy horizon. It stared out, heavy-limbed and satisfied, across its vast, dusty homeland.

The mood is quite calm. I think the lion might have eaten a lot and he's happy that he's had a big meal.

Section 3 — Word Art

© CGP — not to be photocopied

Suggested Scaffolding

Ask pupils to think about the image this creates. Ask them what the words suggest about the lion's appearance, and why he might be 'satisfied'.

Feeling A Little Moody — Aims:

- to investigate with pupils how word choices can influence the mood and tone of writing
- to enable pupils to read examples of mood-setting passages and analyse their effects
- to allow pupils to practise using exciting vocabulary to set the mood for their own writing.

29

The length of sentences a writer uses can have a big effect on the mood too. Read this text.

Was anyone there? He couldn't hear a thing... He took two steps forward. If only he could see something... Anything... Two more steps. He felt he was close now... One more step...

What do you notice about the structure of this passage? How does it contribute to the mood of the text?

Don't forget... structure also includes sentence length and punctuation.

The author has used short sentences and ellipses. The short sentences speed up the action. The use of ellipses creates a feeling of suspense.

A typical ghost story might feature a creepy old house haunted by ghosts, but using the same old settings and characters can make your stories predictable and a bit dull. Write your own ghost story, but try to make it as <u>unpredictable</u> as possible. You'll still need to use scary adjectives, dramatic verbs and an exciting structure though!

Here are a few ideas to get you started: a creepy circus controlled by a zombie ringmaster, a doll factory infested with spiders, or a family of vampires that live in an abandoned football ground.

Bee crouched behind a row of seats in the circus tent, her knees trembling and her breath bursting in her lungs. Suddenly, a shadowy figure limped into the centre of the ring, one leg dragging through the sawdust. She heard the electrifying sound of a whip cracking and the lights above her snapped on. Slowly, the zombie ringmaster turned his gruesome head towards Bee...

How can you create different moods in your writing?

I can choose my words carefully, use dramatic verbs and change the length of my sentences.

Extra Background

Ellipses (e.g. "one more step...") can be used to show a character's frantic behaviour and to build tension.

Suggested Scaffolding

Pupils may wish to retell a story that they know well, focusing on adding exciting vocabulary to change the mood. They can then change the ending, add a character, or add a plot twist. This keeps the focus on vocabulary and refining the mood and tone, rather than spending too much time planning the story.

Pupil Guidance

Pupils can be shown how to maintain pace by portraying action through dialogue. E.g. '"It can see you, Bee!" hissed Alan.', instead of 'Alan realised that the zombie could see Bee.'

Poem Palettes!

30

Poem Palettes!

Poetry is about turning your thoughts and feelings into a piece of art. You choose words carefully and precisely, like artists choose colours to put on their palettes.

Let's think about the process of creating a poem. In the poem below, 'The Door' by Miroslav Holub, the writer thinks about what might be behind a door. Read the poem, and think about the images he uses, and the message he is giving the reader.

The Door

Go and open the door.
Maybe outside there's
A tree, or a wood,
A garden,
Or a magic city.
Go and open the door.
Maybe a dog's rummaging,
Maybe you'll see a face,
or an eye,
or the picture
of a picture.
Go and open the door,
If there's a fog
It will clear.
Go and open the door.
Even if there's only
The darkness ticking,
Even if there's only
The hollow wind,
even if
nothing
is there,
go and open the door.
at least
there'll be
a draught.

The poet repeats some words and phrases. Circle them on the poem, then explain why you think the poet repeats them.

✎ I think the poet repeats these words to add some structure to the poem. I think the words 'maybe' and 'even if' make you think.

Now look at the images he uses for what might be behind the door. Do you think the order of the images matters?

✎ Yes, because first it's about places, then a dog and a face, then some fog and then nothing, so the things are getting smaller.

What would you say is the message of the poem?

✎ You should explore things because you don't know what you might find.

Poem Palettes! — Aims:

- to consider how a poet builds up words and phrases to create an effect
- to allow pupils to choose words which they would like to add to a personal vocabulary
- to enable pupils to create a poem, selecting both personal and appropriate vocabulary.

All of this book has been about words. Look back through the book for any words or phrases that you like or that have seemed important to you. Add them to your word palette below.

pirouetted

flowering vegetation

bedazzle   budgerigar

boomerang

we shall fight   lily-livered

Suggested Scaffolding

If pupils struggle to get started with this task, suggest that they look for groups of words, e.g. words that are fun to say, words that have interesting spellings. This would also provide them with a starting point for the next question.

Are any of these words connected? Do any of them talk about a similar feeling or an idea? Group all your similar words together.

You could have a group of words that sound similar, or a group of words with similar meanings.

action words

pirouetted

we shall fight

bedazzle

words I like to say out loud

budgerigar

lily-livered

boomerang

formal words

flowering vegetation

pirouetted

budgerigar

Extension Idea

Dictionaries and thesauruses can be used to find the meaning of unknown words, and to add extra words to each group.

Now look at the words and phrases that you have written down above. Write them out on a separate piece of paper, and cut them up. Shuffle them around and re-arrange them. Have you found a poem yet? You'll probably want to repeat some of them, and add some other phrases.

When you're happy with your poem, write it out onto a piece of paper. What is the message of your poem? How have you communicated your message?

It's about opening the door to my Year 7 classroom. I used 'maybe' a lot because I'm a bit nervous about it.

Suggested Scaffolding

There are several ways of generating ideas for this task. You could base it on the idea of a door again, asking pupils to imagine what might be behind a classroom door, a dungeon door, a secret door etc. Alternatively, they could draw ideas from the words they have chosen, seeing if they can put together any adjectives, nouns and verbs to make phrases to get them started.

Section 3 — Word Art

Pupil Guidance

Pupils can be told that lots of poetry can have private meanings, so they don't have to share this answer if they don't want to.

Powerful Puzzlers

Extra Background

Spoonerisms were named after a lecturer called William Spooner, who kept mixing up his words. His students thought that this was very funny.

Suggested Scaffolding

Write out the words, cut the first letters off, and re-arrange them so the phrase makes sense. Then see if any spelling changes are needed.

Extension Idea

Pupils might like to make a collection of spoonerisms to put on the walls of the classroom. They could add their own, and collect any others that they hear.

Pupil Guidance

Encourage pupils to think of phrases they know well, and mix them up.

32

Powerful Puzzlers

There are so many ways to make people laugh,
But have you ever tried spoonerisms? They're more fun by half!
They happen when you mix up the letters in words,
To create the strangest sentences you'll ever have heard!

<u>Spoonerisms</u> happen when the first letters of words end up all mixed up.

Keep your pies eeled $\implies$ Keep your eyes peeled

Try to figure out what these spoonerisms really mean.

You have hissed all my mystery lessons. ➡ You have missed all my History lessons.

A well-boiled icicle. ➡ A well-oiled bicycle.

Wave the sails. ➡ Save the whales.

Can you make up your own spoonerisms for these phrases?

I hit my funny bone. ➡ I hit my bunny phone.

It's pouring with rain. ➡ It's roaring with pain.

What a crushing blow! ➡ What a blushing crow!

Now think up your own spoonerisms. How many can you make? Write them in the box below and see if your teacher can work them out.

Why are you fighting a liar? (Why are you lighting a fire?)
I was so dirty I had to shake a tower. (I was so dirty I had to take a shower.)

Try speaking to a friend just using spoonerisms.
Can they figure out what you're saying?

Powerful Puzzlers   *© CGP — not to be photocopied*

Extension Idea

Pupils could create a story with a character who mixes up their words. Not everything the character says needs to be a spoonerism.

E6WPT21